D1442619

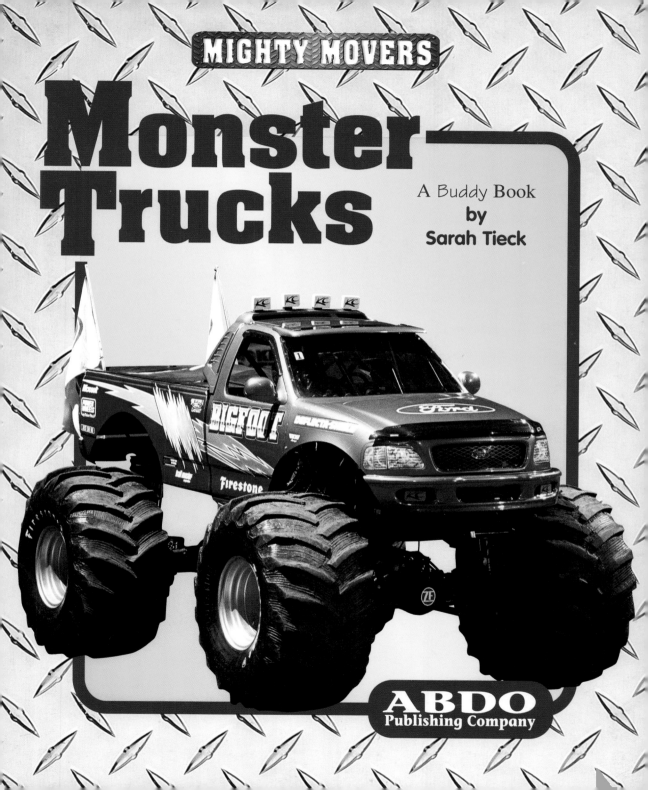

VISIT US AT
www.abdopub.com

Published by ABDO Publishing Company, 4940 Viking Drive, Edina, Minnesota 55435.

Printed in the United States.

Written and Edited by: Sarah Tieck
Contributing Editor: Michael P. Goecke
Graphic Design: Maria Hosley
Image Research: Sarah Tieck
Photographs: BIGFOOT 4x4, Clear Channel Motor Sports, Scott Coldiron, Corbis, Medio Images
BIGFOOT® is a registered trademark of BIGFOOT® 4x4, Inc., 6311 N. Lindbergh Blvd., St. Louis, MO 63042

Library of Congress Cataloging-in-Publication Data

Tieck, Sarah, 1976-
  Monster Trucks / Sarah Tieck.
      p. cm. — (Mighty movers)
  Includes index.
  ISBN 1-59197-829-7
      1. Monster Trucks—Juvenile literature. I. Title.

TL230.15.T55 2004
796.7—dc22

                                          2004050246

Table of Contents

What Is A Monster Truck?

A monster truck is not like other trucks. The monster truck's engine is loud. The engine roars like a monster.

A monster truck isn't like the four-wheel-drive trucks on the street. It is about 11 feet (3 m) tall and 12 feet (4 m) wide. It drives on tires that are 66 inches (168 cm) tall. It weighs about 10,000 pounds (4536 kg).

Monster trucks are not allowed on city streets.

It can take as long as a year to build a monster truck. The cost to build one is about $150,000 to $250,000. The cost to run a monster truck is about $120,000 per year.

Monster truck parts are made to be strong.

BIGFOOT

Bigfoot was the original monster truck. Bob Chandler and his wife, Marilyn, built Bigfoot. The Chandler family business is called Midwest Four Wheel Drive and Performance Center. Bigfoot helped their business grow.

Today, Bob and Marilyn Chandler own about 18 Bigfoot trucks. These trucks appear in events, movies, and races.

What Do Monster Trucks Do?

There are about 300 monster trucks in the United States. Some of these monster trucks compete all over the country. They want to see which truck is the strongest.

Drivers show off skills like jumping at events.

People watch monster trucks crush junk cars, race, or drive on off-road tracks.

Monster trucks also jump off ramps. They can go as high as 25 feet (8 m) in the air. The monster truck's wheels are tall. Its wheels crush junk cars.

Monster trucks can go up to 80 miles (129 km) per hour.

Every monster truck has a different design.

Monster trucks have names. Some of their names are Grave Digger, Samson, and Bigfoot.

Monster Truck Parts

Monster trucks are built using a frame. This frame is called a chassis. It holds the truck's parts together. It also helps protect the driver.

Monster trucks go very fast for a short time. Their engines have more horsepower than regular trucks. Horsepower is a way to measure how fast an engine goes. Most cars have about 140 horsepower. Monster trucks have 1,500 to 2,000 horsepower.

Every truck's body and chassis are custom built. This means that no two are the same.

History Of Monster Trucks

1974—Bob and Marilyn Chandler started the monster truck craze. They built a truck named Bigfoot.

1982—Bigfoot crushed junk cars for a crowd. This was the first "car crush".

1982-1984—More monster trucks were built. The monster truck drivers flattened junk cars at events.

1984—Monster trucks started racing each other.

1987—Eleven monster truck owners and drivers started the Monster Truck Racing Association.

December 1987—Forty-nine people attended the first meeting of the Monster Truck Racing Association. The Monster Truck Racing Association worked to make the sport safe.

1989–1992—Dan Patrick designed a new style of chassis. This chassis made monster trucks lighter. Most monster trucks still use this style of chassis.

Monster trucks have changed since 1974.

Safety And Monster Trucks

Monster trucks drive fast. Monster trucks jump off ramps. Sometimes they crash or roll over.

Monster trucks have parts that help keep people safe. All the drivers wear gloves to protect their hands. They also wear a harness. This is a special seat belt. The drivers protect their heads with helmets. They wear a brace around their necks. Special clothes protect the drivers from fire.

A harness is a special seat belt that helps keep drivers safe. It is padded and goes over both shoulders for added safety.

Most trucks have several switches to turn their engine off. They make it possible for a truck to be shut off fast in case of an emergency. This keeps the driver and the crowd safe. The driver has one. There is one on the back of each truck, too. Also, a member of the crew has a remote control switch to turn off the truck.

Each monster truck has a fire extinguisher.

Sometimes monster trucks roll over.

Monster Trucks Today

Many people go to see monster trucks race. There are more than 700 monster truck events each year in the United States. The people who build monster trucks work to make them safe and fun for everyone.

Important Words

compete to take part in a race or event where someone is the winner.

crew a group of people who work together.

engine a machine that creates energy to make something run or move.

four-wheel drive truck a truck with power in all four wheels. This is also called a 4x4 truck.

harness a special seatbelt with many padded straps to hold the driver in.

off-road track a special racetrack with rocks, dirt, and hills.

Web Sites

To learn more about monster trucks, visit ABDO Publishing Company on the World Wide Web. Web site links about monster trucks are featured on our Book Links page. These links are routinely monitored and updated to provide the most current information available.

www.abdopub.com

Index